THE WORLD AT WAR
WORLD WAR II

Life as a
Combat Soldier

Heinemann
LIBRARY

. . . . Brian Williams

www.heinemann.co.uk/library
Visit our website to find out more information about **Heinemann Library** books.

To order:
☎ Phone 44 (0) 1865 888066
▤ Send a fax to 44 (0) 1865 314091
▢ Visit the Heinemann Bookshop at www.heinemann.co.uk/library to browse our catalogue and order online.

First published in Great Britain by Heinemann Library, Halley Court, Jordan Hill, Oxford OX2 8EJ, part of Harcourt Education.
Heinemann is a registered trademark of Harcourt Education Ltd.

Editorial: Andrew Farrow and Dan Nunn
Design: Lucy Owen and Tokay Interactive Ltd (www.tokay.co.uk)
Picture Research: Hannah Taylor and Sally Claxton
Production: Duncan Gilbert

Originated by Repro Multi Warna
Printed and bound in China by WKT Company Limited

The paper used to print this book comes from sustainable resources.

ISBN 0 431 10378 X
10 09 08 07 06
10 9 8 7 6 5 4 3 2 1

British Library Cataloguing in Publication Data
Williams, Brian, 1943–
    Life as a Combat Soldier. – (World at war. World War II)
    1. Great Britain. Army – History – Juvenile literature 2. World War, 1939–1945 – Great Britain – Juvenile literature
    I. Title
    940.5'41241
A full catalogue record for this book is available from the British Library.

Acknowledgements
The publishers would like to thank the following for permission to reproduce photographs:

AKG-Images p. **15**; Corbis pp. **4** (Hulton Deutsch Collection), **5** (Bettmann), **7** (Bettmann), **8** (Bettmann), **9** (Swim Ink 2, LLC), **10 top** (Hulton Deutsch Collection), **11** (Bettmann), **13** (Bettmann), **14 bottom** (Hulton Deutsch Collection), **16** (Bettmann), **17** (Bettmann), **19 top** (Hulton Deutsch Collection), **20** (Hulton Deutsch Collection), **21**, **22** (Bettmann), **23 top right** (William A. Bake), **24** (Hulton Deutsch Collection), **23 bottom** (Bettmann), **27 top** (Bettmann), **27 bottom** (Hulton Deutsch Collection), **28** (Michael St Maur Sheil); Getty Images pp. **6 bottom** (Time & Life Pictures), **10 bottom** (Hulton Archive); Popperfoto p. **19 bottom**; Topfoto.co.uk pp. **6 top**, **12** (Roger-Viollet), **23 top left** (UPP); Topham Picturepoint pp. **18**, **25**; TRH Pictures pp. **14 top**, **26**.

Cover photograph of US infantry advancing in France reproduced with permission of Corbis/Bettmann.

Every effort has been made to contact copyright holders of any material reproduced in this book. Any omissions will be rectified in subsequent printings if notice is given to the publishers.

CONTENTS

Some words are shown in bold, **like this**. You can find out what they mean by looking in the glossary.

A NEW WAR BEGINS

In 1939, the German Army invaded Poland. World War II had begun. For the next six years, soldiers of many nations went into combat, to fight. Millions were killed or wounded.

In the 1930s, the **Nazis** came to power in Germany. The Nazis believed in military might. Their leader, Adolf Hitler, had fought as a combat soldier in World War I. Hitler promised to make Germany strong again, with a new army. Many people, **civilians** as well as army **generals**, supported him, and lots of young men joined the German Army or *Wehrmacht* to train as soldiers.

Hitler invades Poland

On 1 September 1939, Hitler sent his soldiers to invade Poland. Britain and France had promised to defend Poland, and told Germany to stop its attacks. Hitler ignored them. On 3 September, the British prime minister, Neville Chamberlain, broadcast the solemn news by radio: Britain was at war with Germany.

▲ German troops advance through Poland. By 1939, Germany had a modern army with tanks supported by bomber planes. The Poles fought bravely, but could not stop the Nazi **Blitzkrieg** (German for "lightning war").

By 1940, the Germans had overrun much of Europe. Even though it had Europe's biggest army, France was defeated. Britain and its **Commonwealth** partners, including Australia and Canada, fought on. The United States was still at peace when, on 7 December 1941, Japan attacked the US naval base at Pearl Harbor, in Hawaii. This surprise attack brought the United States into the war.

April 1939	1 September 1939	3 September 1939
End of the Spanish Civil War, in which some German soldiers gain combat experience.	German troops attack Poland. The Polish cavalry are no match for German tanks.	Britain and France go to war with Germany. Italy joins the war on Germany's side in 1940.

▲ In 1939, the United States was reluctant to get involved in a new war. In December 1941, however, Japanese aircraft made a surprise attack on US warships in Pearl Harbor. The United States was now at war. The raid showed how effective air power could be, against targets at sea or on land.

Soldiers from many nations

To fight this global war, millions of men and women left their homes and peacetime jobs to join the army. Many never came home again, for World War II killed more people than any war in history. At least 17 million men and women died while serving in the armies, navies, and air forces. This book will tell you how combat soldiers were trained and how they fought in the biggest war in history.

May and June 1940	**22 June 1941**	**7 December 1941**
Germany overruns Holland, Belgium, and France. In June, over 300,000 British and French troops are rescued from Dunkirk.	German armies invade the Soviet Union (Russia). By Christmas, they have nearly reached the Russian capital city, Moscow.	Japanese naval planes attack Pearl Harbor. The United States enters the war.

Pr paring for w r

The war was not a surprise to most people. They believed that countries like Germany, Italy, and Japan threatened world peace. By 1935, factories in many countries were busy making new guns, tanks, aircraft, and ships for their armed forces. The world was rearming – making its armed forces stronger. As war loomed closer, thousands of young men were **conscripted** (drafted or "called up") to train as soldiers.

◀ Trenches are dug in London parks in 1938, as Britain gets ready for war. Before 1939, politicians like Winston Churchill had urged the British government to rearm more quickly. Peace campaigners argued that more guns and more soldiers would only make a new war inevitable.

Slide towards war

Even before it went to war, the US Army began calling up men. By the summer of 1939, British and French reserve troops (ex-soldiers who had returned to civilian jobs) were back in uniform. Experienced soldiers showed new **recruits** how to fill sandbags, dig trenches, and put on **gas masks**. Many families had sad memories of World War I (1914–1918), in which millions of soldiers had been killed. They feared this new war would be worse. In 1939, some leaders told people the war would soon be over. But soldiers quickly realized this new war was going to last years.

▶ German volunteers fought for General Franco's Fascists in Spain's civil war (1936–1939). In Spain, these volunteers tried out new tactics and weapons.

How armies grew

- In 1939, France had Europe's biggest army: 5 million men

- Germany had around 4 million

- Britain's army had only 430,000 men, including reserve troops

- the US Army was even smaller, 190,000 men

- but by 1945, Britain's army had grown to 2.9 million...

- ...and the US Army numbered 8.3 million.

7

In the News

"Every male aged 18 [to 41] is required to register at the Labour Exchange. You will be called for a medical examination. If you pass, you will receive a letter of conscription and a rail warrant [ticket] from the local station to the assigned barracks [army base]."

What the British government told young men receiving "call-up papers".

▶ New recruits take an oath of loyalty before joining the US Army. Most had never lived away from home before. Some were excited, but almost all were scared and homesick too.

Eyewitness

Don Ellingworth was a British Army despatch rider (motorcycle messenger) when war broke out. He noticed a change as he rode around the army town of Aldershot. "...people were shouting and waving, something they'd never done before. Before the war the army was not much thought of, but after 11 o'clock on 3 September 1939 the army was something wonderful." *Quoted in* Pillar of Fire *by Ronald Atkin (Sidgwick and Jackson, 1990)*

L ARNING Tu IGHT

LEARNING TO FIGHT

All soldiers had to learn to fight. Some German and Japanese soldiers had fought in combat before 1939. Few British or American soldiers had been in battle since World War I. They had to learn fast.

About a third of the German army was made up men over 40 years old, who had fought in World War I. Britain and America had some veterans too, but most of their soldiers were young men who had either volunteered or been conscripted for military service. They travelled by train to an army camp to begin their army lives.

Off to camp

Basic training took around six weeks. It was hard work. All soldiers looked forward to free time, when they could relax, play cards, listen to records, or read letters from home. Even better was time off, called leave or furlough.

Joining a regiment

After basic training, soldiers joined a **regiment**. Some became **infantry** (foot-soldiers), others were sent to fire **artillery** (big guns), or crew tanks and other armoured vehicles. Some became paratroopers (parachute soldiers). Not all new soldiers became front-line combat troops. Many were trained to do the other jobs the army needed – they became cooks, communications specialists (called signallers), medics, drivers, engineers, mechanics, police, and clerks.

▲ Drill sergeants taught recruits how to march, fire their guns, and keep their weapons clean. Recruits also practised marching, until they were ready to parade in front of their commanding officer with their new rifles.

January 1940
Britain calls up all men aged 20 to 27 for military service.

June 1940
German troops study English phrase books, as they train for an invasion of Britain.

29 October 1940
In the United States, conscription is enforced in peacetime, for the first time in US history.

▶ Government posters called on young men and women to join the army. This poster appeared in the United States.

COURAGE AND GALLANTRY IN ACTION

INFANTRY
UNITED STATES ARMY

Army traditions

New soldiers were taught about army life. Some units were proud of traditions going back hundreds of years. The Scottish regiments of the British and Canadian armies, for example, marched to the stirring tunes of bagpipes. But as well as loyalty to their regiment, many soldiers, especially in the US Army, felt the strongest bonds with their comrades or "buddies" – perhaps people from their home state or town.

Women in the army

Women's branches of the armed forces were started. Many women joined the army and wore uniforms, but they did not fight as combat soldiers in the Allied or German armies. There were women fighters in the Soviet Army and in **Resistance** groups in **occupied** countries.

18 November 1940	Dec 1941 – May 1942	26 January 1942
First soldiers conscripted under the new draft law join the US Army.	Japanese troops capture Hong Kong, the Philippines, and Singapore.	Troopships land US soldiers in Britain – the first US troops to land in Europe since World War I (1914–1918).

Basic training

The US Marines called it "boot camp". This was the base where every new soldier's training began. Military discipline came as a shock to many recruits. First they lined up to collect their uniform, boots, helmets, and other kit. The next thing they learned was that soldiers were constantly being given orders, which had to be obeyed instantly. They ate army food and slept in army beds, as many as 30 men to a barrack room. They soon learned to keep their beds and kit tidy for inspection – or get into trouble.

Army life

Most men soon got used to army life. Every day started early with "Reveille" (a wake-up call). Soldiers washed and shaved in a communal bathhouse. They ate together in the mess hall or canteen, usually grumbling about the cooking. To get fit, they did physical training exercises and also "route marches" and cross-country runs, sweating under the weight of equipment and weapons. "We were toughened up. We learned to scrub a garbage can [dustbin] until you could see your face in it, make your bed so tight a quarter [coin] would bounce on it", was how one American soldier remembered training.

▲ British soldiers practise using their bayonets during training in 1942. On the assault course, soldiers scaled walls, swam rivers, crawled through drains, and climbed up ropes. They also practised fighting battles using real bullets.

▶ A soldier's kit included boots, uniform, sewing kit, razor for shaving, mug and cooking pot, as well as a weapon. New soldiers learned to polish their boots and the metal buttons on their uniforms.

▲ American soldiers on a "high-stepping" assault course in Virginia, in the United States, in 1942. This exercise taught them how to cross obstacles as they marched through the jungle.

Ranks in armies

- Most new soldiers began as private soldiers (privates), the lowest rank, taking orders from non-commissioned officers or NCOs (corporals and sergeants).

- Above the NCOs were the commissioned officers – beginning with lieutenants and going up through captain and major to colonel.

- At the top of the chain of command were generals and (in the British, Russian, and German armies) field marshals.

Eyewitness

"One of the NCOs handed you a slip of paper with a number. This was your personal identification number. You had to remember it, because without it you did not exist." *Most World War II soldiers could still recall their army numbers 40 or 50 years later!*

GOING TO WAR

Army training made soldiers proud to belong to a team and taught young men a strong sense of loyalty.

Soldiers fought in groups or units. The numbers varied between armies, but the smallest unit was a squad of around 10 men. Next came a platoon (between 16 and 40 men), a company (about 200 men), a battalion (up to 1,000 men), a brigade (5,000 men), and finally a division (15,000 or more). Each man was trained to obey orders instantly, and help his comrades. Soldiers received extra training before being sent to fight in snowy mountains, desert, or jungle. Some learned special fighting skills too.

On foot and on wheels

Infantry soldiers fought on foot, though at times they rode on trucks or half-tracks (trucks with caterpillar tracks for extra grip). Mechanized units had armoured cars or tanks, whose crews included a driver, gunner, and commander. Transport units had trucks and jeeps, while engineers drove bulldozers, heavy rollers, and diggers.

Big guns and rockets

Artillery soldiers or gunners fired field guns and **howitzers**. These were so heavy that they often had to be towed by trucks. A big gun needed a gun crew of from five to eight men. Allied soldiers respected the German 88 mm gun, which could blow up a tank a mile away. Some artillerymen fired ear-shatteringly loud rockets, in screeching clusters of smoke and flame.

▲ Soldiers accompany a tank as the **Allies** advance across Normandy in 1944. The invasion of France on D-Day was the biggest invasion in history, involving millions of soldiers, sailors, airmen, and others.

April 1940	Sept 1941	December 1941
British troops land in Norway to resist the German invasion, but soon have to withdraw.	German troops begin the siege of Leningrad. The Russian city is besieged until January 1944.	US troops go into action against the Japanese in battles for Guam and Wake Island.

From air and sea

Airborne troops or "paratroops" were trained to jump from planes, wearing parachutes. Navy soldiers, or **marines**, went to sea in warships and often made the first landings on enemy-held coasts. Other soldiers were taught to come ashore from ships or in smaller boats called **landing craft**. **Commandos** and **Rangers**, trained to raid enemy territory, were skilled in hand-to-hand combat and in using explosives.

Far from home

When Allied soldiers went to war, they had to cross the oceans – to Europe, North Africa, India, or the Pacific. Often men did not know where they were going until they got there. As they steamed away in a troopship, they had no idea when they would see their homes and families again.

▲ These US Marines are leaving their landing craft, small boats that were unloaded from bigger transport ships. Once close to shore, the Marines waded or swam onto the beaches, usually under heavy enemy fire.

Crossing the ocean

During the war, the luxury ocean liners *Queen Mary* and *Queen Elizabeth* were converted to troopships. Each ship carried over 10,000 US soldiers at a time across the Atlantic Ocean to Britain. The men slept four to a cabin. More than one million soldiers made the six-day crossing in this way.

October 1942	2 February 1943	6 June 1944
Battle of El Alamein in North Africa is a much needed Allied victory, after a string of defeats.	A German army surrenders at Stalingrad in Russia. 100,000 Germans are dead. 90,000 are taken prisoner.	D-Day. 39 Allied divisions (20 US, 14 British, 3 Canadian, 1 Polish, 1 French) land in France.

A soldier's weapons

GOING TO WAR

A combat soldier had to fight to protect his life and the lives of his friends. To do this, he depended on his weapons.

Rifles and machine guns

An infantry soldier carried a **rifle** or a carbine (a gun like a rifle, but with a gas-powered firing mechanism). Some soldiers had pistols or revolvers (small hand-held guns). The US M-1 carbine weighed 2.5 kilograms (5.5 pounds), about half the weight of a British Lee-Enfield rifle. The **range** of a rifle was between 500 and 1,800 metres (1,640 and 5,905 feet). Some rifles fired one shot at a time, while others, such as the US Browning, fired a short burst of bullets every time the soldier squeezed the trigger. The soldier loaded his gun with a **magazine** holding between 10 and 30 bullets, or rounds.

▲ An American infantryman with his M-1 carbine, the standard US weapon during World War II.

Machine guns fired a stream of bullets very quickly. The German MG 42 spat out 1,200 rounds a minute. Some soldiers carried lightweight sub-machine guns like the Thompson ("Tommy gun"). Heavy machine guns rested on metal legs while being fired.

▶ British machine-gunners training in gas masks. Heavy machine guns were hidden in holes or concrete bunkers, but lighter guns could be carried by one soldier. Machine-gun fire was deadly to troops caught in the open – on a beach, for example.

Eyewitness

The success of soldiers and of armies depended a great deal upon the quality of their weapons. A British soldier noted the poor condition of the Italian army in North Africa.

"Much of the artillery dated from the Great War (1914–1918). The tanks were poor. We felt nothing but pity for Italian soldiers who went out to fight in what were mobile sardine tins..."

Other weapons

- The bazooka was a hand-held rocket launcher, able to blow a hole in concrete or a tank's steel armour.

- Soldiers threw grenades – small bombs.

- Mortars looked like upright, hollow tubes; they lobbed shells up in the air to fall on enemy positions.

▲ A German officer instructs a soldier firing an anti-tank weapon.

Eyewitness

American troops fought hard in Italy in 1943. Here is a description of one encounter, involving US Army captain Benjamin Butler.

"...he [a fellow-soldier] rose up quickly in his hole and fired. His automatic rifle chattered and spewed out its clip of twenty bullets as he swung it back and forth. In his foxhole, Butler heard the mortars thumping the ground all around him. A sound like a sudden soft wind meant the falling shells were dangerously close..." *From Battlefire! by Col. Arthur Kelly (The University Press of Kentucky, 1997)*

FIGHTING OVERSEAS

Soldiers fought in deserts, tropical jungles, and the freezing Russian winter. Sometimes special kit was provided, but often men had to make the best of what they had.

Winter battles

On the **Eastern Front**, Russian soldiers felt the harsh weather (nicknamed "General Winter") was on their side. Oil and petrol froze in fuel tanks, so trucks and planes could not move. Tanks got stuck in mud and snow, and supply convoys were bogged down, bringing the German advance to a halt. Most Russian troops had thick snow-clothing, but many thousands of German soldiers froze to death because they had no winter kit.

▲ In the Russian winter, both sides suffered terribly. Unlike the Russian soldiers pictured here, the German soldiers were not equipped for a winter war. This was because they had invaded in summer, without snow-clothing.

The desert war

In North Africa, the problem was heat. From 1941 to 1943, German and Italian armies fought Commonwealth troops in battles across the desert. Soldiers endured scorching sun, sandstorms, dust, and flies. In the desert, water was even more important than fuel. Troops sweated in the heat of the day, and shivered during the chill of night. Trucks often broke down when their engines became clogged with sand.

January 1941	June 1941	August 1942
British and Australian troops defeat the Italian army in Libya.	German armies attack Russia, hoping to reach Moscow before winter. By December they are halted just a few miles from the city.	A German army attacks the Soviet city of Stalingrad but is defeated by January 1943.

Tank war

Tanks played a key part in the battles in Russia and North Africa.

- Most tanks had one big gun and several smaller guns.

- World War II tanks weighed from 20 to 70 tons, and rumbled along at speeds of 32–64 kph (20–40 mph).

- The best tanks, like the Russian T-34 and German Panther, had such thick armour that infantry found them hard to "knock out".

- Only other tanks, planes, and anti-tank guns could smash a big tank attack.

▲ These Australian soldiers in the North African desert are "dug in", in a trench fortified with sandbags for extra protection.

Dressed for the desert

Soldiers adapted their kit for desert life. Most Commonwealth troops and many Germans wore shorts during the day, though Italians and most Americans stuck to long trousers. Floppy hats and caps replaced tin hats: the Australian "bush-hat", with its wide brim, was a favourite. Troops of the special patrol units, who ranged far across the desert in jeeps and trucks, copied the local people's clothes and headgear to help keep cool.

Soldiers learned to cope with desert life. The men of the British 7th Armoured Brigade, who helped win the Battle of El Alamein in 1942, were proud to call themselves the "Desert Rats".

A general's opinion

In August 1942, Britain's prime minister, Winston Churchill, appointed General Bernard Montgomery to lead the 8th Army in the North African desert. The general asked one soldier, "What is your most valuable possession?" "My rifle, sir," he said. "No, it isn't, it's your life," replied "Monty".

June–October 1942	8 November 1942	July 1943
The German *Afrika Korps* advances towards Cairo, Egypt. Commonwealth troops win the Second Battle of El Alamein.	140,000 Allied troops land in Morocco and Algeria to help drive German and Italian forces from North Africa.	Huge tank battles near Kursk in Russia end in a German defeat.

In the jungle

Some of the fiercest fighting of World War II took place in the jungles of Asia and the Pacific islands. Many Allied soldiers thought the Japanese must be expert in jungle warfare. This was not true. Most Japanese soldiers knew as little about the jungle as an Australian from Sydney or a Welshman from Cardiff. But they never questioned an order, and made do with simple, rugged equipment. Japanese soldiers could march 32 kilometres (20 miles) a day, living on a daily ration of 1.8 kilograms (4 pounds) of food (mainly rice). Allied soldiers also learned to cope with jungle life, often living in terrible conditions for weeks away from their base. There were very few good roads, so mules and horses were often used for carrying supplies.

Eyewitness

"They just stayed where they were and kept firing..."

Allied soldiers were shocked that Japanese troops seemed not to care how many were killed. Nor did they surrender, because they thought it cowardly. This was why some Japanese ill-treated Allied prisoners of war. Japanese soldiers usually fought to the last man.

▲ Japanese soldiers on the march. Most Japanese troops were infantry soldiers. They were trained to cover long distances on foot, carrying their weapons, kit, and food.

Jungle kit

In the jungle, every soldier carried:

- ammunition (bullets) in pouches and belts

- rations (food) and a canteen of drinking water

- a small shovel to dig a shelter-hole

- a bayonet, knife, or machete, to hack a path through jungle, and a rifle.

◀ Standard-issue uniforms made from wool and cotton cloth were uncomfortable in tropical heat and when wet. Shorts were no good either – they gave little protection from biting mosquitoes. This US soldier is pictured wearing jungle camouflage gear instead. The outfit included a mosquito mask, high rubber shoes, a poncho, and camouflage trousers.

Hat with many uses

Each army had its own style of helmet or "tin hat". The US army helmet (right), as one soldier recalled, could be used as a "wash-basin, cooking pot, emergency latrine [toilet], digging tool, and even a weapon at close quarters." The net cover was useful for sticking in leaves and twigs as **camouflage**.

ATTACK AND RETREAT

In the great battles of World War II, attack and victory were often followed by defeat and retreat.

German Blitzkrieg

Between September 1939 and May 1940, German armies defeated most of their enemies in what became known as *Blitzkrieg* (German for "lightning war"). The French Army was defeated. British troops retreated to the French port of Dunkirk, from where more than 300,000 men were rescued by ships and taken to England. Their tanks, guns, and other equipment were left behind. In the summer of 1940, Britain's "Home Guard" of old men and volunteers stood ready to fight alongside the army if the Germans invaded. But then Hitler sent his armies to invade the Soviet Union in 1941.

▲ German soldiers attack a French farmhouse during their *Blitzkrieg* on France in 1940. Within a few months, France had surrendered.

America shows its strength

In the Pacific war of 1941–1942, Japanese soldiers too knew victory after victory, capturing the Philippines and drawing near Australia. But by 1943, American factories were pouring out ships, planes, and guns. Millions of new soldiers were being trained. Germany, Italy, and Japan could not match this growing strength.

On the Eastern Front, the Russians drove back German armies. In 1943, Allied troops landed in Italy. By 1944, the Allies had assembled a vast invasion force in England for the D-Day invasion of France on 6 June. The battle that began on D-Day became a turning point of the war.

1941–1942	13 October 1943	24 December 1943
The Japanese advance in Asia, towards Australia. The Allies are forced to retreat.	Italy changes sides and declares war on Germany, after the Allied invasion of Italy.	Dwight D. Eisenhower is chosen to be supreme commander of the Allied invasion of France.

US troops come ashore on the Normandy beaches after the D-Day landings. The Allies poured in men and machines to secure their toehold on the French coast.

Eyewitness

Fred Bentley, a British soldier, crossed to Normandy on D-Day.

"I've never seen anything like it ... as far as you could see nothing but boats and boats. They looked like stepping stones ..."

The D-Day landings

The Allied commander, American General Eisenhower, knew the Germans would fight hard. The invasion force had to get ashore, smash through the German defences and establish a base or "bridgehead". On D-Day, more than 150,000 troops waded from landing craft onto the beaches of Normandy, France. With them came tanks, trucks, and guns. Other soldiers parachuted in. Fighting was fierce, especially on Omaha Beach where the Americans suffered heavy **casualties**. But the beaches were secured, and as the days passed, thousands more soldiers, tanks, and guns were landed.

By the end of 1944, France and Belgium had been freed. Allied troops crossed the River Rhine into Germany, and Russian troops advanced from the east. In spring 1945, German soldiers, many of them teenagers, fought the last battles of the war in Europe, with fighting raging in the streets of Berlin.

21

6 June 1944	23 August 1944	March–June 1945
"Operation Overlord" begins on D-Day. The battle for Normandy lasts until the end of July.	Allied troops enter Paris, led by the French 2nd Armoured Division.	US forces capture the islands of Iwo Jima and Okinawa, but suffer heavy casualties as the Japanese defend their homeland.

Casualties of war

In a battle such as the Normandy invasion, a soldier was lucky if he was not killed or wounded. As soldiers waited to go into action, most were scared. They pulled on their tin hats a little tighter, took a deep breath, maybe said a quick prayer, and made for the beach.

On D-Day, some soldiers splashed ashore with hardly a shot fired at them. But at Omaha Beach, many US troops were killed in the water and on the narrow strip of beach. They frantically dug "foxholes" to shelter from bullets and shell-bursts. Even after the Allies pushed inland, the fighting was still fierce. In the Normandy countryside, soldiers dashed through holes they had hacked in the hedges, but many were shot down by German fire as they tried to cross fields.

Eyewitness

Paul Mudd (age 19) of the US 35th Infantry Division landed in Normandy in July 1944. He was soon in action.

Sheltering in a hedge, he found a badly wounded US sergeant. Paul gave first aid and stuck the sergeant's rifle in the ground, as a marker for the medics. Then he had to push on, thinking that his war "had gotten off to a bad start".

▲ Germans taken prisoner by the Allies. On D-Day, German troops were shelled by Allied warships, bombed by Allied planes, and then faced wave after wave of troops and tanks. As they lost ground, most German soldiers knew that the war was now lost.

Prisoners of war

Thousands of soldiers were taken prisoner and questioned. A captured soldier was required to say only his name, army number, and rank. There were international rules about the humane treatment of **prisoners of war (POWs)** but they were not always followed. Thousands of German POWs in Russia died of hunger and cold. Many Allied POWs died of ill treatment in Japanese prison camps.

▧ Soldiers receive medals for brave actions in battle. The highest military honours included the British Victoria Cross (far left), and the US Congressional Medal of Honor (left) and Purple Heart. Men killed in action were awarded **posthumous** decorations. The dead soldier's family received the medal.

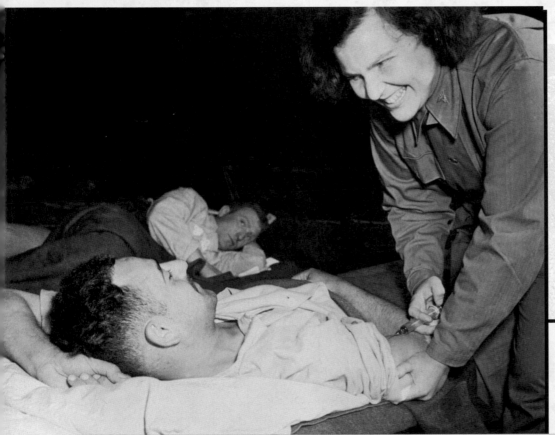

Eyewitness

"Many wounds were infected ... which meant **amputation**. Fortunately we saved many lives by the injection of penicillin ..."

A nurse in Normandy in 1944 was thankful for penicillin, the new "miracle antibiotic" drug.

▲ Wounded men were given emergency first aid on the battlefield by army medics. They were then moved to emergency first-aid stations and from there to hospital. Badly wounded soldiers were sent home to recover. Men with less serious wounds returned to the fighting when they were passed fit again.

SPECIAL FORCES

Some soldiers volunteered to take part in dangerous raiding missions. These "special forces" included Commandos, Rangers, and the Special Air Service (SAS).

The British Army formed its first Commando unit in 1940. Soldiers who volunteered to be Commandos went through extra-tough training for "combined operations" – missions using ships and soldiers. There were also French, Dutch, Norwegian, and Czech Commandos, and the US Rangers trained in a similar way.

Only the toughest...

Only the toughest soldiers passed the physical tests to get into the special units. They were taught to find food and shelter in the countryside, to climb cliffs, and swim rivers. They were trained to use all kinds of weapons, from knives to rocket-launchers. Special forces landed by boat to raid enemy-held coasts, or made secret patrols behind enemy lines to blow up key targets such as fuel dumps or airfields.

▲ Dashing through fire was only part of the training received by these US Rangers. They were supposed to be able to overcome any obstacle.

Behind enemy lines

Regular soldiers and marines also prided themselves on making long expeditions into enemy-held territory. In 1943, British general Orde Wingate's band of "Chindits" spent four months in the jungles of Burma, raiding the Japanese. A US unit called "Merrill's Marauders", after their leader Brigadier-General Frank Merrill, fought in the jungles of Burma in 1944.

24

March 1941

In the first British "combined operations" raid, British Commandos raid the German-held Lofoten Islands, off the coast of Norway.

1942

Col. William O. Darby forms the first US Rangers unit of 2,000 men trained in Britain for Commando-style operations.

March 1942

British Commandos raid St Nazaire, France, damaging a submarine base and sinking a destroyer to block the dry dock.

▶ Officers of the British Long Range Desert Group in North Africa. Formed in June 1940, its patrols (of 20 men in 5 vehicles) raided behind enemy lines.

Secret operations

Two famous special units were the British Special Air Service, or SAS, and the Australian Independent Companies. Trained in secret, these soldiers were often sent on top secret missions and sometimes disappeared behind enemy lines for weeks. The motto of the SAS was "Who dares, wins"!

Eyewitness

"Anybody would be a fool to try this ... It was crazy then ..." said Lt Col. James Rudder looking up at the crumbling Normandy cliffs in 1954. It was ten years since D-Day, when he led the 2nd US Rangers ashore in Normandy.

Dangerous jobs

In 1944, the 2nd US Rangers were given a very dangerous mission: to climb the steep cliffs at Pointe du Hoc, west of Omaha Beach, and destroy six German guns. On 6 June, the Rangers scrambled up to find no guns – only telephone poles made to look like guns. The guns had been moved into an orchard. In the two-day fight to put the guns out of action, 81 of 225 Rangers died and most of the others were wounded.

25

August 1942	1942–1943	6 June 1944
In an "invasion rehearsal", Allied troops, mostly Canadian, land at Dieppe in France. But the raid fails and many Canadians are killed or captured.	US Marines train Raiders battalions for Commando attacks on Japanese-held islands in the Pacific.	2nd US Rangers storm the cliffs at Pointe du Hoc during the D-Day landings in Normandy.

Special gear

Special forces used a mixture of standard infantry weapons (such as carbines, sniper rifles, machine guns, and mortars). But their training included unarmed combat, stalking, explosives, and **sabotage** (such as the best way to blow up a railway).

Fighting hand-to-hand

Commandos and Rangers were trained to sneak up on an enemy guard silently and disarm or immobilize him quickly. Keeping silent meant they could not use guns. So the men learned martial arts – fighting with their bare hands, a knife, or a cosh (a club or even a sock filled with sand).

Before every mission, a soldier checked his kit and weapon, making sure his gun was in perfect working order. It might save his life, or those of his comrades.

Special weapons

Some Commandos and Rangers were armed with special weapons:

- sniper rifles with telescopic sights, for shooting at long range

- grenades with short time-fuses set to explode almost immediately

- plastic explosives that could be stuck in place on a target, such as a fuel tank

- petrol bombs that burst into flames

- "sticky bombs" made by stuffing a sock with explosive and covering it with grease to stick to the metal side of a tank.

▶ Commandos and Rangers trained for sea landings from small boats and landing craft. For climbing cliffs, they used ropes, metal ladders in sections, and rocket-propelled grapnels (claws with ropes attached), which they fired to the top of the cliff.

Eyewitness

Charles Moore commanded a "Phantom Patrol" of ten men who parachuted into France in June 1944 with the SAS. The Phantoms' job was to contact the French Resistance, sabotage roads and railways, and disrupt German troop movements, to aid the D-Day landings. For three months the Phantoms used top-secret radios and **carrier pigeons** to send reports. They used biscuit tins filled with sand and burning petrol as flares (lights) to guide Allied planes dropping their supplies.

▲ US Ranger Thomas R. Nabors of Nashville, Tennessee, poses with his weapons in 1944. Like many members of the special forces, he had volunteered because he wanted to "see some action".

◀ Special forces were sent on sabotage missions, sometimes alongside Resistance fighters. They would set explosive charges to blow up a railway track or damage a factory.

EACETIM

In 1945 the war ended with joyful celebrations. Millions of soldiers handed in their weapons and left camp for the last time. Many prisoners of war and wounded men came home and faced years of slow recovery. Some combat soldiers found it hard to adjust to peacetime life. Back with their families, ex-soldiers returned to their old jobs or looked for new ones.

The soldiers' sacrifice

The young men who fought the battles of World War II are now old. Each year on 11 November (Veterans' Day in the United States, Armistice Day in Britain and many other countries), soldiers remember their comrades. Visitors read the names on war memorials and stare at the lines of war graves in World War II military cemeteries, from Normandy to Okinawa. So many names remind us of the sacrifices brave soldiers made. The familiar phrase "For your tomorrow, we gave our today" sums up what they did.

Eyewitness

"You can't help thinking of the pals you've left behind in the jungles of Burma or on the beaches of those Pacific islands."

Lieutenant Frank Palmer, a British prisoner of war.

Military casualties in World War II

Australia 23,000

Britain 264,000

Canada 37,000

Germany 3.5 million

Italy 242,000

Japan 1.3 million

New Zealand 10,000

United States 292,000

USSR 11 million

▲ Veterans kept in touch with wartime friends and, as the years passed, old enemies became friends too. In June 2004, German veterans stood alongside British, French, Canadians, Americans, and others to remember D-Day, on the 60th anniversary of the invasion of France.

TIMELINE

1939

1 September Germany invades Poland. World War II begins.

3 September Britain and France declare war on Germany.

1940

January All men aged 20–27 face conscription in Britain.

April Germans invade Denmark and Norway.

May Germans invade Belgium, Netherlands, and France.

June France surrenders. Germans march into Paris on 14 June.

May–June More than 300,000 Allied troops are rescued from Dunkirk.

July Britain prepares for invasion. Regular troops are backed up by volunteers of the Home Guard.

July–September Battle of Britain – German air force tries to defeat Britain's air force so German army can invade Britain.

September All Americans aged 21–35 must register for military service.

October First US conscripts join the army, even though the United States is not yet at war.

1941

March US government passes the Lend-Lease Bill to provide military help to Britain and its allies.

April German armies take over Greece and Yugoslavia.

22 June German armies invade the Soviet Union.

7 December Japan attacks Pearl Harbor; more than 2,300 Americans are killed. The United States joins the war. Next day Britain and Canada declare war on Japan.

December Men up to age of 51 now face conscription in Britain.

1942

January First US troops set foot in United Kingdom.

February Japanese troops capture Singapore.

May Manila in the Philippines falls to Japanese forces. Japan's rapid victories threaten Australia.

August US troops land at Guadalcanal, in the Solomon Islands.

August Dieppe raid, in France – many Canadians are lost.

September Germans and Russians fight for Stalingrad (in the Soviet Union). In this battle, 1.3 million men are killed.

October–November Allies win the Second Battle of El Alamein in North Africa.

November Allied troops land in Algeria and Morocco to help drive the Germans and Italians from North Africa.

1943

February A German army surrenders at Stalingrad.

March Australians halt Japanese advance in eastern New Guinea.

May Allies push German and Italian forces out of North Africa.

July–September Allied troops invade southern Italy.

July Huge tank battle at Kursk between Germans and Russians. Two million men and 6,000 tanks take part. Russians win.

October General Stilwell's US-Chinese army marches into north Burma to attack the Japanese.

November US forces land on Tarawa in the Gilbert Islands in the Pacific Ocean.

1944

January Fierce fighting around Monte Cassino monastery in Italy.

April British and Indian troops defeat Japanese at Imphal, close to the Indian border with Burma.

4 June Allies enter Rome, Italy.

6 June D-Day. Allied armies invade France.

20 July A plot by German army officers fails to assassinate Hitler.

25 August Paris is liberated by Allied troops.

September Allies drop paratroops at Arnhem in a bid to capture Rhine bridges, but the plan fails. Allies take the port of Antwerp in Belgium.

October US forces begin recapture of the Philippines in the Pacific.

1945

January Soviet troops enter Auschwitz, the Nazi death-camp in Poland.

February US Marines storm Iwo Jima island. Manila in the Philippines is liberated. Japanese are in retreat from Burma.

March US and British armies cross the Rhine into Germany.

April Soviet troops attack Berlin. On 30 April Hitler kills himself.

April Fierce fighting on Okinawa island between US and Japanese soldiers.

2 May Berlin is captured by Soviet armies.

7 May Germany surrenders.

8 May VE (Victory in Europe) Day. End of the war in Europe.

June Okinawa captured; 160,000 Japanese are killed; US losses are over 12,000.

6 and 9 Aug Allies drop atomic bombs on Hiroshima and Nagasaki. Japanese stop fighting.

14 August V-J (Victory over Japan) Day marks the end of the war in the Pacific.

29

GLOSSARY

allies nations joining together to fight an enemy. The Allies in World War II included the United States, Britain, the USSR, France, Australia, Canada, New Zealand, South Africa, and other Commonwealth countries.

amputation removal of an arm or leg

artillery large guns firing shells

Blitzkrieg German for "lightning war", fast attacks made by tanks and ground troops, supported by aircraft

camouflage disguise that makes something blend in with its surroundings, such as painting a tank like sand in the desert

carrier pigeon pigeon that flies home with a message fastened to its leg

casualties people killed or wounded in battle

civilians people who are not in the armed forces

Commandos soldiers trained for surprise raids

Commonwealth countries with special links to Britain, as members or former members of Britain's empire

conscripted ordered by law to join the army

dysentery bad infection causing stomach trouble, diarrhoea, and dehydration

Eastern Front name given to the Russian-German front

gas mask breathing apparatus to protect a person from poison gas

general senior officer in the Army

howitzer a cannon which fires shells high into the air

infantry soldiers who fight on foot

landing craft boat used to ferry soldiers from a ship to the shore

magazine snap-in holder with bullets, loaded into a gun

malaria disease spread by mosquitoes

marines soldiers trained to fight from ships

Nazis members of Hitler's National Socialist German Workers' Party

occupied taken over by an enemy army

posthumous happening after someone has died

prisoners of war (POWs) soldiers captured while fighting and held in prison camps

range distance a gun can fire a bullet or shell

Rangers US commando-type soldiers

recruits people who have just joined the armed forces or any organization

regiment army unit made up of battalions and companies

Resistance organized groups fighting an "underground war" against an occupying enemy

rifle standard long-barrelled gun

sabotage wrecking factory machines or communications to hinder an enemy

FINDING OUT MORE

If you are interested in finding out more about World War II, here are some more books and websites you might find useful.

Further reading

Your local public library's adult section should have plenty of war books, with first-hand accounts by soldiers who fought in North Africa, in Europe and in the Pacific. Written by people who were actually there, such books will give you an idea of what combat soldiers thought about the war and their part in it.

Books for younger readers

Causes and Consequences of the Second World War, Stewart Ross (Evans, 2003)

Causes of World War II, Paul Dowswell (Heinemann Library, 2002)

Going to War in World War II, Moira Butterfield (Franklin Watts, 2001)

History Through Poetry; World War II, Reg Grant (Hodder Wayland, 2001)

The Day the War was Won, Colin Hymion (Ticktock Media, 2003)

World in Flames: On Land, Neil Tonge (Macmillan Children's Books, 2001)

WW2: The Allied Victory, Sean Sheehan (Hodder Wayland, 2000)

WW2 True Stories, Clive Gifford (Hodder Children's Books, 2002)

Also the Heinemann Library *Holocaust* series (several titles).

Websites

http://www.iwm.org.uk/ – the website of the Imperial War Museum in London.

http://www.wartimememories.co.uk/ – a website containing wartime recollections, including those of people who fought on the front line.

http://bbc.co.uk/history/war/wwtwo/ – this website from the BBC has lots of resources about World War II.

INDEX

Titles in the *World At War* series include:

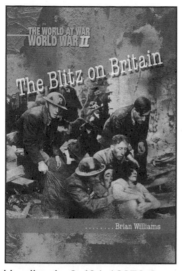

Hardback: 0-431-10376-3

Hardback: 0-431-10380-1

Hardback: 0-431-10377-1

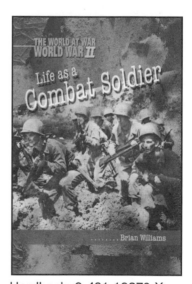

Hardback: 0-431-10378-X

Hardback: 0-431-10379-8

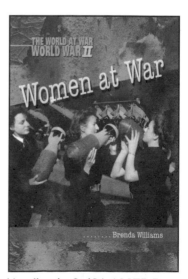

Hardback: 0-431-10375-5

Find out about other titles from Heinemann Library on our website www.heinemann.co.uk/library